FACES IN STONE

ARCHITECTURAL SCULPTURE IN NEW YORK CITY

W. W. NORTON
NEW YORK · LONDON

FACES IN STONE

ARCHITECTURAL SCULPTURE IN NEW YORK CITY

ROBERT ARTHUR KING

FOREWORD BY ALLISON SILVER

MAPS BY ALICE THIEDE

This book is dedicated to six influential women in my life:

Neva B. Simon, Casey L. Thomas, Rachel A. King, Marisa L. Simon, Jennifer L. King, and Elinor M. King

Also, in memory of a loyal, honest, and true friend, Rick Johnson

Previous pages: see page 104.

Printed in Singapore
First Edition

For information about permission to reproduce selections from this book, write to Permissions,
W. W. Norton & Company, Inc., 500 Fifth Avenue, New York, NY 10110

For information about special discounts for bulk purchases,
please contact W. W. Norton Special Sales at specialsales@wwnorton.com or 800-233-4830

Manufacturing by KHL
Book design by Eleen Cheung
Production manager: Leeann Graham

Library of Congress Cataloging-in-Publication Data
King, Robert Arthur, 1945–
Faces in stone : architectural sculpture in New York City / Robert Arthur King ; foreword by Allison Silver.
p. cm.
ISBN 978-0-393-73234-4 (hardcover)
1. Decoration and ornament, Architectural—New York (State)—New York. 2. Sculpture—New York (State)—New York. 3. New York
(N.Y.)—Buildings, structures, etc. I. Title.
NA3511.N48K56 2008
729'.5—dc22
2007044819

W. W. Norton & Company, Inc., 500 Fifth Avenue, New York, N.Y. 10110
www.wwnorton.com

W. W. Norton & Company Ltd., Castle House, 75/76 Wells Street, London W1T 3QT

2 4 6 8 0 9 7 5 3 1

PREFACE

⁓⁂⁓

"The creation of art is not the fulfillment of a need but the creation of a need." —Louis I. Kahn

This book started years ago as a photography class assignment that just grew and grew. The assignment was to photograph women. I don't like photographing people, so my solution was to take the photos of women's faces on buildings. The instructor was surprised by my end run around his request, but pleased with the results.

The assignment focused my attention on building details all over New York City, and I spent hours over the next few years recording faces, finding them more and more intriguing. Who carved or sculpted these details? Why? Did the faces represent specific people?

Sometimes research provided answers. For example, the faces on the Woolworth Building, 229-237 Broadway, include the owner, the architect, and the builder. Their visages will remind observers of their existence as long as the building stands! The building at 45 Monroe Street displays the face of the developer, a signature for his work. Sometimes the sculptures depict the children or family members of the property owner—for example, at 120 Riverside Drive, Manhattan, and 156 Prospect Park West, Brooklyn. Other sites recognize particular types rather than individuals: the carvings on the Montauk Club, 25 Eighth Avenue, Brooklyn, are Native Americans, specifically members of the Montauk tribe from the tip of Long Island.

Most of the buildings with sculpted decorative details were built during the years between the Civil War and World War I, a period that included the storied Gilded Age, when an influx of European emigrants, among them many skilled craftsmen, provided the wherewithal to embellish the dwellings and businesses of newly affluent citizens. The ornate and sometimes ostentatious details were designed for entrances, around doorways, on cornices, and in lobbies. Classic Greek and Roman images were particularly popular. The wonderful ornamentation, whether beautiful women's faces or frightening grotesques, or natural elements such as acanthus leaves, vines, and flowers, was intended to impress visitors and residents, and still does.

Many of the buildings so decorated have been torn down, but many remain for the observant to enjoy. Their condition ranges from the well maintained to the derelict. Only serious attention by concerned citizens will save the most vulnerable ones. If taste, style, and cost have eliminated such architectural detail from modern architecture as indicated by the current prevalent blank-faced, repetitive buildings, there is all the more reason to salvage and preserve for posterity the legacy left to us by the profoundly talented but largely anonymous craftsmen whose work we admire so much.

THE FACES THAT YOU MEET

by Allison Silver, Politics Producer, Charlie Rose

Though the prototype of the modern city, New York is decidedly Old World. For example, it is ideal for pedestrian traffic. It is also a metropolis of soft watercolors, not the hard Day-glo colors of other New World cities like Los Angeles or Las Vegas or Miami. Rather, New York's Beaux-Arts behemoths and stately brownstones are designed in muted colors and sepia tones.

These buildings are old-fashioned, steadfast structures, built on rock-solid foundations. They hearken back to the Gilded Age, the bustling Gotham of ruthless plutocrats proclaiming their legacy, substantial burghers asserting their prosperity, and working-class strivers struggling for a toehold—a New York not unlike that of today.

Yet these stolid buildings, seemingly so sturdy and impassive, are often adorned with fantastical beings, carved out of stone or molded in terra cotta that call out to modern passersby, telling of the New York of dreams, a city of wonder and enchantment.

They are storied creatures from another time: fauns and nymphs, satyrs and naiads, conquistadors and Native Americans, gods and goddesses. They testify to a magical city where anything is possible—where a shoeshine boy can become a titan of industry, a nimble storyteller an influential novelist, a shy small-town girl the sophisticated toast of the town. They speak to the myths that drew people to the city, myths that create a great city.

A real city, we know, is always about change: people are transformed in the cauldron of the melting pot. Yet these ornamental faces who watch over the change are eternal and immutable, from long-told tales. In a city where little stays the same, they do. They are hidden in plain sight, on capitals and plaques, capstones and cornices. They seem to offer age-old wisdom as they survey the fast urban pace, yet remain apart from it.

The faces shown here are New World variations on gargoyles. They are not gargoyles in the traditional meaning of that word. True, many have their mouths open, wildly laughing or crying (in a sort of precursor to painter Edvard Munch's "Scream" series), but these are not fanciful downspouts for rainwater. They are not there to ward off evil. Most are grotesques or humoresques, with misshapen or idiosyncratic, exotic or whimsical faces. Still others are beautiful women with classic features and serene (if stony) brows. Many of the faces, even those so clearly depicting late nineteenth- or early twentieth-century tycoons, are framed by swirls of cascading curls. Some are crowned with laurel wreaths. Venerable gentlemen have remarkable beards or assertive mustaches. Sweet-faced children are frozen, unmoving in a most unchildlike manner. Specific artists are memorialized, painters such as Rembrandt and Whistler. And, on Riverside Drive, all the arts of the city are honored—a chef as well as a painter, an architect, a carpenter.

Some figures have a syncopated, Jazz Age feel—like a remarkable visage on Broome Street, peaking out from a machine-age motif. Others are as neoclassical as profiles on a Roman coin. Still others are pre-Raphaelite, dreamy and ethereal. They surprise and delight—Hercules in his lion's skin is no less expected than Teddy Roosevelt.

The faces can appear randomly or surreptitiously. You are walking along when, suddenly, you spot a face laughing down or grimacing out at you. Then, the most mundane of buildings becomes extraordinary—dashing or natty or elegant.

In a city, they say, you can be lonely, but never alone. You are always one among many. But look at this another way. One of the joys of New York is that, in so many neighborhoods, on so many different streets, even when no other people are around, you are forever a face in the crowd.

Note: Unless otherwise specified, addresses are in Manhattan.

For maps showing the location of the faces and an index to the addresses, see pages 142-144.

106 Prospect Park West, Brooklyn

Subway: **F** Bus: **B69**

Map #2

502 12 Street, Brooklyn

Map #6

25 Eighth Avenue, Brooklyn

Subway: ② ③ Bus: B41, B67

Map #13

Map #60

480 Park Avenue

Subway: 4 5 6 N R W
Bus: M30

Map #49

Map #1

521 12 Street, Brooklyn

Subway:  F   Bus: B69

Map #8

429 3 Street, Brooklyn

Map #14

485 13 Street, Brooklyn

Subway: **F** Bus: B69, B75

Map #7

584 11 Street, Brooklyn

Map #9

121 Prospect Park West, Brooklyn

Subway: **F** Bus: B69

Map #3

Map #80

816 Eighth Avenue, Brooklyn

Subway:  F   Bus: B69

Map #10

Map #5

371 East 138 Street, Bronx

Subway: **6** Bus: BX15, BX33

Map #1

218 St. Ann's Avenue, Bronx

Map #2

1 Park Avenue

Subway: **6** Bus: M1

Map #39

Map #50

198 Eighth Avenue, Brooklyn

Map #11

202 Eighth Avenue, Brooklyn

Map #12

165 Orchard Street

Map #30

375 Broome Street

Subway: J M Z Bus: M103

Map #23

7 Elizabeth Street

Subway:  Bus: M103

Map #20

Map #34

25 Henry Street

Subway: F Bus: M15, M22

Map #3

13 Division Street

Map #17

26 Jefferson Street

Map #6

16 West 125 Street

 Subway: **2** **3** Bus: M100, M101

Map #87

9 Henry Street

Subway: F J M Z

Bus: M15

Map #2

Map #11

27 Rutgers Street

Subway: **F** Bus: M22

Map #13

35 Henry Street

Map #3

58 East 1 Street

Subway: F V Bus: M15

Map #31

43 West 105 Street

Map #73

45 Monroe Street

Subway: **F** Bus: M15, M22

Map #1

52 Mott Street

Subway: Bus: M103

Map #19

56 Henry Street

Subway: **F** Bus: M22

Map #4

15 Eldridge Street

Map #16

Map #28

73 Eldridge Street

Subway: Ⓑ Ⓓ Bus: M15

Map #26

75 Central Park West

Map #59

76 West 85 Street

Subway: **B** **C**   Bus: M7, M11

Map #66

78 West 85 Street

Map #66

2154 Frederick Douglass Boulevard

Subway: **B** **C** Bus: M7, M10, M116

Map #81

96 East Broadway

Map #15

104 Forsyth Street

Subway: **B** **D** Bus: M15

Map #27

156 Prospect Park West, Brooklyn

Map #4

111 Henry Street

Subway: **F** Bus: M15, M22

Map #5

Map #72

310 St. Nicholas Avenue

Subway: A B C D Bus: M3

Map #86

Map #70

121 Henry Street

Map #5

129 West 86 Street

Subway: 1 B C
Bus: M7, M11, M86

Map #67

Map #67

Map #76

130–132 Eldridge Street

Subway: Bus: M9

Map #29

Map #56

162 Henry Street

Subway: **F** Bus: M15, M22

Map #5

376 Lafayette Street

Map #33

Map #25

Map #5

173–185 Fifth Avenue

Subway: R W 6 Bus: M1, M2, M3

Map #36

181 Mott Street

Subway:
Bus: M103

Map #22

211 Madison Street

Subway: **F** Bus: M22

Map #12

Map #14

201 West 79 Street

Map #63

Map #68

191 Henry Street

Subway: F Bus: M22

Map #9

205 West 77 Street

Subway: **1** Bus: M7, M11

Map #61

221 Madison Street

Subway: **F**   Bus: M22

Map #10

223 Madison Street

Subway: **F** Bus: M22

Map #10

239 Central Park West

Subway: **B** **C** Bus: M10

Map #64

Map #8

250 West 77 Street

Map #62

251 East Broadway

Map #7

255 West 108 Street

Subway: **1** Bus: M4, M60, M104

Map #78

Map #95

Map #98

102 Edgecombe Avenue

Map #98

260 Convent Avenue

Subway: ① Ⓐ Ⓑ Ⓒ Ⓓ

Bus: M18, M100, M101

Map #90

284 Fifth Avenue

Subway: 6 R W
Bus: M2, M3, M5

Map #38

4 East 39 Street

Subway: 4 5 6 7
Bus: M1, M2, M3, M4, M5

Map #41

315 Park Avenue South

Subway: **6** Bus: M1

Map #37

Map #44

341 West 122 Street

Subway: Bus: M3, M10

Map #84

362 Broome Street

Map #21

368 Convent Avenue

Subway:  Ⓐ Ⓑ Ⓒ Ⓓ

Bus: M18, M100, M101, BX19

Map #92

370 Park Avenue

Subway: 6 E V
Bus: M1, M2, M3

Map #43

Map #53

527 West 134 Street

Subway: **1** Bus: M100, M101

Map #88

473 West 145 Street

Subway: Ⓐ Ⓑ Ⓒ Ⓓ

Bus: M18, M100, M101, BX19

Map #91

390-394 Broome Street

Map #24

411–413 Fifth Avenue

Subway: 6 B D F V N R W Q
Bus: M2, M3

Map #40

418 Convent Avenue

Map #93

5 Elizabeth Street

Map #20

440–448 Ninth Avenue

Map #47

443 West 135 Street

Map #89

450–454 Avenue of the Americas

Subway: Ⓐ Ⓑ Ⓒ Ⓓ Ⓔ Ⓕ Ⓥ ① Bus: M5, M6

Map #35

452 Fifth Avenue

Subway: B D F V 7
Bus: M2, M3

Map #42

463 Seventh Avenue

Subway: 1 2 3 Bus: M10, M20

Map #45

Map #18

475 West 145 Street

Subway: Ⓐ Ⓑ Ⓒ Ⓓ

Bus: M4, M5, M18, M100, M101, BX19

Map #91

540 Manhattan Avenue

Subway: Ⓐ Ⓑ Ⓒ Ⓓ   Bus: M3, M18

Map #85

495 West End Avenue

Subway: **1** Bus: M5

Map #69

521 West 145 Street

Map #94

523 West 134 Street

Map #88

527 Cathedral Parkway

Subway: ① Bus: M4, M11

Map #79

Map #52

557 Eighth Avenue

Map #46

285 Central Park West

Map #65

644 Broadway

Subway: ⑥ Ⓑ Ⓓ Ⓕ Ⓥ

Bus: M1, M6

Map #32

778 Park Avenue

Map #55

2495–2499 Adam Clayton Powell Boulevard

Subway: **3** Bus: M2, BX19

Map #96

Map #71

Map #71

909–917 Columbus Avenue

Subway: **1** **B** **C** Bus: M7, M11, M16

Map #74

Map #97

925 West End Avenue

Subway: **1** Bus: M5, M104

Map #77

1947 Adam Clayton Powell Boulevard

Map #82

912 Amsterdam Avenue

Subway: **1**   Bus: M7, M11

Map #75

Map #51

Map #83

1377 Lexington Avenue

Subway: **4** **5** **6**
Bus: M98, M101, M102, M103

Map #58

1534 Third Avenue

Subway: ④ ⑤ ⑥
Bus: M98, M101, M102, M103

Map #57

927 Fifth Avenue

Subway: **6** Bus: M1, M2, M3, M4

Map #54

1221 York Avenue

Subway: 6 F Bus: M31

Map #48

Map #83

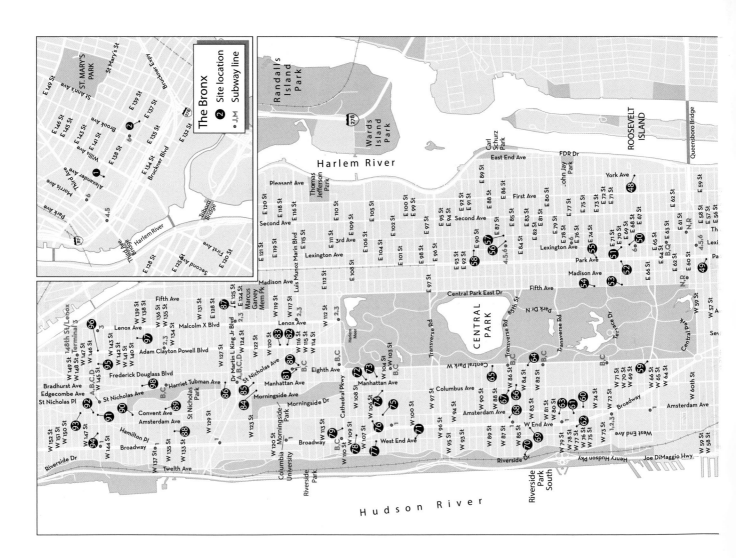

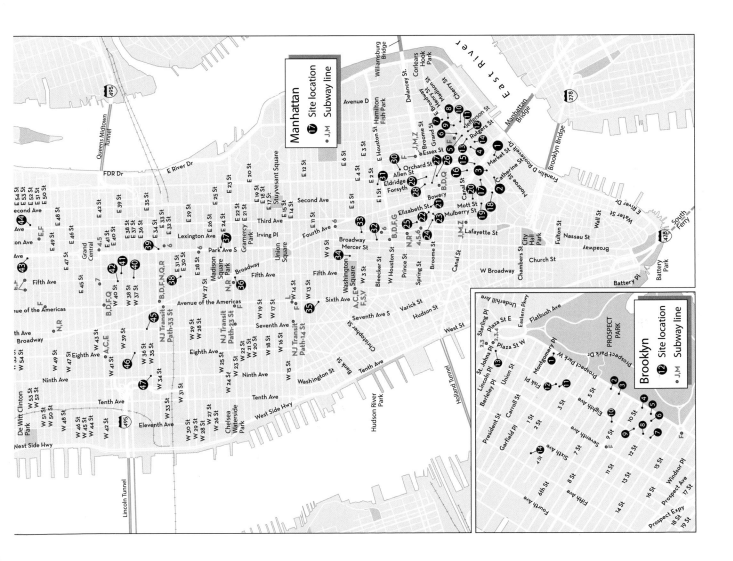

ACKNOWLEDGMENTS

꽃

I thank those who have suffered the walks with me in search of building detail, Elinor M. King, Jennifer Huang, and Tamera M. Gamble, as well as my two best friends, Jacqueline G. Perry and Derryck W. Brooks-Smith, who have listened to me for hours expressing my enthusiasm for architectural details throughout the city.

INDEX

꽃